The Jackson Chronicles

by

JAMES JACKSON

Unless otherwise noted, scriptures are taken from the King James Version Bible. Scripture quotations marked.

REL109010 RELIGION / Christian Education / General

ISBN-9798733698540

DEDICATION

This book is dedicated to the late Alice L. Jackson, my wife of 31 years, who went to be with the lord May 10, 2020. She was a strong woman of God who always loved and encouraged me to be the best for both Jesus and my family.

Table of Contents

God's Decision

WHEN GOD CREATED THE UNIVERSE, HE SAID LET
THERE BE LIGHT.

IT WASTED NO TIME BEFORE IT CAME INTO SIGHT.

THE HOLY SPIRIT WAS THERE HELPING TO CARRY
THE PLAN OUT.

FAITH WAS IN THE PLAN OF CREATION AND THAT IS
NO DOUBT.

GOD SAID AND SAW BY FAITH WHAT HE WANTED IT
TO BE.

HE CREATED THE FOWLS OF THE AIR AND ALL THAT
IS IN THE SEA.

THE STARS, MOON, SUN, AND FIRMAMENT IN THE SKY
HE CALLED HEAVEN.

GOD MADE ALL CREATION IN SIX DAYS AND RESTED
ON DAY SEVEN.

EVERYTHING GOD MADE WAS IN HIS HEAVENLY
PLAN.

BUT HIS GREATEST CREATION WAS WHEN HE MADE
MAN.

1.3.1995

The Price Has Been Paid

THE PRICE HAS BEEN PAID AND THE
FOUNDATION HAS BEEN LAID.
THE PRICE WAS JESUS'S BLOOD WITH
WHICH ENTRANCE TO HEAVEN WAS
MADE.
THE PRICE HAS BEEN PAID AND NOW
WE HAVE THE FREE GIFT.
THE BLOOD WAS THAT PRICE AND A BURDEN WE
DON'T HAVE TO LIFT.
THE PRICE HAS BEEN PAID AND SALVATION IS NOW
FREE.
THE PRICE THAT THE BLOOD PAID WAS FOR ALL
HUMANITY.
THE PRICE HAS BEEN PAID IN FULL, NOW ALL WE
HAVE TO DO
 IS RECEIVETHE FREE GIFT THAT MAKES ALL THINGS
NEW.
THE PRICE HAS BEEN PAID AND IT WAS AN ACT OF
LOVE.
THE PRICE HAS BEEN PAID AND THE FOUNDATION
LAID FROM THE GOD ABOVE.
THE PRICE HAS BEEN PAID, NOW THERE IS A CHOICE
YOU MUST MAKE.
THE PRICE HAS BEEN PAID AND THERE IS NO REASON
TO HESITATE.
THE PRICE HAS BEEN PAID AND THE WORD
PREACHED TO ALL MANKIND
THE PRECIOUS BLOOD OF JESUS WAS SHED SO MAKE
UP YOUR MIND.
THE PRICE HAS BEEN PAID FOR YOU AND THERE IS
NOTHING LEFT.
THE PRICE WAS PAID AND FOUNDATION LAID IF
YOU'RE LOST BLAME YOURSELF.
THE PRICE HAS BEEN PAID, NOW YOU MUST MAKE
THE CALL.
THE PRICE HAS BEEN PAID BY JESUS; NO EXCUSES
CAN BE MADE AT ALL.

2.14.2020

I Have the Wisdom of God

I TRUST GOD TO THE UTTEMOST.
CAUSE I'M FILLED WITH THE HOLYGHOST.

I HAVE THE WISDOM OF GOD

I DON'T CARE WHAT PEOPLE SAY.
I'M GONNA TRUST HIM ANYWAY.
I KNOW WHAT THE WORD SAID.
HE'S THE ONE THAT HUNG AND BLED.

I HAVE THE WISDOM OF GOD

I WILL SET HIS MONEY FREE
CAUSE HE'S THE ONE THAT GAVE IT TO ME.
I WILL NOT LIVE BY PEOPLE'S THOUGHTS.
HE PAID THE PRICE; MY SOUL HE BOUGHT.

I HAVE THE WISDOM OF GOD

THE BLOOD HE SHED FOR OUR LIVES.
WAS NOT FOR THE WORD TO BE COMPROMISED.

I HAVE THE WISDOM OF GOD

HE THAT DIED FOR OUR SIN.
MOVED FROM OUTSIDE TOWITHIN.

I HAVE THE WISDOM OF GOD

SO. RENEW YOUR MIND AND BE SINCERE.
THE RETURN OF JESUS IS DRAWING NEAR.

I HAVE THE WISDOM OF GOD

ONCE ON THE CROSS TO SAVE THE LOST;
NEVER TO BE REPEATED.
ONCE IN THE GRAVE ONCE IN HELL TO TAKE
THE KEYS FROM THE DEVIL HE DEFEATEED.

I HAVE THE WISDOM OF GOD

JESUS IS LORD AND REMAINS THE ONE
ANOINTED.
THE DEVIL IS DEFEATED AND REMAINS
DISAPPOINTED

WHAT ROAD ARE YOU TRAVELING?

WHAT ROAD ARE
YOUTRAVELING?
IS IT THE ROAD THAT SEEMS
SO HARD?
IS IT THE ROAD YOU WERE
TRAVELING BEFORE YOU
TURNED TO GOD?
WHAT ROAD ARE YOU TRAVELING?
IS IT THE ONE YOU THINK WILL COST?
THERE IS A ROAD AHEAD THAT HE DIED AND
BLED FOR; FOLLOW & YOU WONT BE LOST.
WHAT ROAD ARE YOU TRAVELING? DO YOU
KNOW WHERE YOU'RE GOING?
IS IT THE ONE WAY AND DEAD END OF THE
SEEDS YOU HAVE BEEN SOWING?
WHAT ROAD ARE YOU TRAVELING? IS IT THE
HIGHWAY THAT'S SINCERE?
IS IT THE ROAD OF SIGNS &WONDER SINCE
THE TIME OF JESUS IS NEAR?
WHAT ROAD ARE YOU TRAVELING? IS IT A
DIRECTION YOU CAN TRUST?
THE WAY, TRUTH AND LIFE IS THE RIGHT
ROAD FOR US.
WHAT ROAD ARE YOU TRAVELING? IS IT
ONE YOU'VE BEEN ON BEFORE?
ARE YOU ASKING QUESTIONS FOR
DIRECTIONS DOES YOUR LIFE IS NOTHING
MORE?
WHAT ROAD ARE YOU TRAVELING? IS IT
DIRTY AND PAVED WITH SIN?

A ROAD TO SALVATION IF YOU CHOOSE IS
ONE THAT WILL NEVER END.
WHAT ROAD ARE YOU TRAVELING? WHAT
LIFE ON THAT ROAD DO YOU LIVE?
IS IT THE ROAD WITHOUT YOUR PERSONAL
LOAD LEADING YOU TO GOD'S WILL?
WHAT ROAD ARE YOU TRAVELING? IS IT THE
RIGHTEOUS ROAD OR ONE FILLEDWITH SIN?
YOUR DECISION NOW CAN BRING
CONFUSION TO AN END.
WHAT ROAD ARE YOU TRAVELING? IS IT THE
ONE TO THE ALTAR CALL?
STRAIGHT IS THE GATE AND NARROW IS THE
WAY TO CONFESSING JESUS. THAT'S ALL.

Get Out of There

OFFENCE MUST COME THE BIBLE SAID,
AND WE MUST BE AWARE.
IF YOU FIND YOUSELF IN OFFENCE, HURRY,
GET OUT OF THERE.
GET OUT OF THERE, AND REPENT, AND
GET BACK TO THE WORD.
OFFENCES WILL DESTROY YOU IN CASE
YOU HAVE NOT HEARD.
MANY WILL LEAD YOU THERE, AND YOU
WILL NOT BE KNOWING.
MAYBE IT'S BECAUSE OF THE SEEDS YOU
HAVE BEEN SOWING.
WE ALL HAVE BEEN THERE BEFORE, AND
SOME OF US DECIDED TO STAY.
SOME DECIDED TO LEAVE THERE, OTHERS
REMAIN THERE TO DECAY.
THERE IS NO PLACE TO BE, BELIEVE ME
WHEN I TELL YOU.
THE ONES THAT STAYED ARE LOST & THE
ONES THAT LEFT THERE ARE MADE NEW.
OFFENCES MUST COME, BUT DON'T YOU
GO WHERE THEY ARE.
THERE ARE SOME ON YOUR JOB, AT HOME,
AND EVEN RIDING IN YOUR CAR.
JUST PLAY IT SAFE AND LET THE WORD OF
GOD TEACH YOU BETTER.
JUST LEAVE THE SIN OF OFFENCE AND
STAY OUT OF IT ALTOGETHER.

12.19.1994

Honey, Honey, Honey

HONEY, HONEY, HONEY, WHAT ARE YOU
TRYING TO DO?

I'M LOOKING IN THE WORD TO FIND WHAT IS
REALLY TRUE.

HONEY, HONEY, HONEY, WHAT ARE YOU
TRYING TO SAY?

I'M LOOKING IN THE WORD SO I WILL KNOW
WHAT IS THE WAY.

HONEY, HONEY, HONEY, WHAT ARE YOU
TRYING TO FIND?

I'M LOOKING IN THE WORD TO RENEW MY
STATE OF MIND.

HONEY, HONEY, HONEY, WHAT ARE YOU
TRYING TO BE?

I'M LOOKING IN THE WORD SO I CAN BE TRULY
FREE.

HONEY, HONEY, HONEY, WHAT ARE YOU
TRYING TO DEMAND?

I'M LOOKING IN THE WORD SO I CAN BETTER
UNDERSTAND.

HONEY, HONEY, HONEY, WHAT ARE YOU
TRYING TO RECALL?

I'M LOOKING IN THE WORD SO I'LL MISS
NOTHING AT ALL.

4.06.2004

Inventory Time

IT'S INVENTORY TIME, BECAUSE THESE ARE THE LAST DAYS.

IT'S INVENTORY TIME, CONSIDER YOUR WAYS.

IT'S INVENTORY TIME, YOUR LIFE YOU SHOULD CONSIDER.

IT'S INVENTORY TIME, DO YOU WALK IN LOVE? ARE YOU STILL BITTER?

IT'S INVENTORY TIME, AND NO TIME TO PLAY AROUND.

IT'S INVENTORY TIME, ARE YOU PREPARING FOR THE LAST TRUMPET SOUND?

IT'S INVENTORY TIME; TIME FOR YOU TO LOOK WITHIN.

IT'S INVENTORY TIME, TO JUDGE YOURSELF OF SIN.

IT'S INVENTORY TIME, WHAT ARE YOU NOW DOING?

IT'S INVENTORY TIME, IS IT JESUS YOU'RE AFTER OR A CAREER YOU'RE PURSUING.

IT'S INVENTORY TIME, TIME TO RETURN TO THE MAN.

IT'S INVENTORY TIME, TIME TO BE TRUE TO GOD, CREATOR OF THE REDEMPTIVE PLAN.

11.30.1996

American Politics

We as Americans, need to get off the political party ride.
We need to stop being biased about race & riches and get on God's side.
We all have heard your lies, about what you'll do if elected.
Then when you win, you pretend, and your memory becomes selective.
The voters are looking for a candidate of truth, one willing to lose their position by telling the truth and standing firm regardless of their critics' opposition.
Some people read about the candidate's name, who they are voting for.
The problem is the readers and the ones they study are way under par.
So how is it that we expect to get the best candidate to win? When we only wait to vote and say it's that time again.
We the American people, must study more than just the ten commandments.
We must have someone in political office who will uphold our constitutional amendments.
The modern American politician in whom hardly no one wants to believe, who only visits the neighborhood when running for office, then lies and waits to deceive.
As Americans we must understand that politics today is a different game. Because of selfish motive, and the heart of the ones in office is not the same.
One of the major issues in America's elections is people that choose not to vote.
Making excuses about it will do no good when they are the scapegoat.
Progress is moving forward and leaving your excuses behind.
Thinking your vote won't do any good is a negative state of mind.
Let us get something straight before we go to the polls.
Study the candidates, pray and vote, but let god take control.

2.07.2020

Dark Youth Revised

STURDY I STAND WITH BOOKS IN MY HAND
TODAY I'M A DARK CHILD BUT TOMORROW I'M A
STRONG MAN.

THE HOPE FOR MY RACE IS TO MOLD A PLACE IN
AMERICA'S BEAUTIFUL LAND.

AN AMERICAN AM I AND NONE CAN DENY, AND
HE WHO OPPRESSES ME IT IS HIM I DEFY.

I AM DARK YOUTH SEEKING THE TRUTH OF A
FREE LAND BENEATH A GREAT SKY,.IT WAS
LONG AGO AT THE NATION'S START BUT YEARS
AGO IN THE HEART THAT ATTUCK DIED

THAT RIGHT ABIDES TO STRENGTHEN OUR
LAND TO IMPART, SO TO BE WISE AND STRONG
YOU MUST STUDY LONG TO SEEK THE
KNOWLEDGE THAT'S RIGHT ALL WRONG

THAT'S MY MISSION, AND TO LIFT MY RACE TO
ITS RIGHTFUL PLACE UNTIL BEAUTY AND
CONCERN FILL EACH DARK FACE IS MY
AMBITION, SO I CLIMB TOWARD TOMORROW
OUT OF PAST SORROWS TREADING THE MODERN
WAY WITH THE WHITES & THE BLACKS OF
NOTHING I'LL HOLD BACK FOR I AM DARK
YOUTH OF TODAY.

3.01.2020

Bless Nature

BLESS THE WIND FOR IT BLOWS

BLESS THE SUN FOR IT SHINES

BLESS THE MOON FOR IT GLOWS

BLESS THE RAINBOW FOR IT'S LINES

BLESS THE STARS FOR THEIR ANGLES

BLESS THE SKY FOR IT HOLDS

BLESS THE EARTH FOR IT'S RECTANGLES

BLESS THE WATER FOR IT FLOWS

BLESS THE RAIN FOR IT FRUITS

BLESS THE SNOW FOR IT FALLS

BLESS THE SEED FOR IT ROOTS

BLESS NATURE'S VOICE WHEN IT CALLS

11.04.1982

LIFE

LIFE IS PRECIOUS AND RARELY APPRECIATED,
SOME THINK THEY HAVE ARRIVED, OTHERS
THINK THEY HAVE GRADUATED.
LIFE IS LOVE AND WE NEED TO DO MORE THAN
JUST THINK ABOUT IT.
LOVE IS PRICELESS & WE NEED TO DO MORE
THAN JUST TALK ABOUT IT.
LIFE IS ABOUT LOVING HUMANITY& WHILE
THEY ARE ON THIS EARTH.
LIFE IS ABOUT LOVING ALL FROM THE WOMB TO
ACTUAL BIRTH.
LIFE IS MORE THAN THE VALUE WE PLACE ON
OURSELVES.
WE MUST REALIZE THERE ARE OTHERS
INVOLVED IN LIFE AS WELL.
LIFE IS ABOUT CHARACTER BUILDING AND NOT
JUST ANOTHER DISCUSSION.
LET US LEARN OUR DUTY OF LOVE AND NOT
SUFFER THE REPERCUSSION.
LIFE IS A GIFT TO YOU AND SHOULD BE PASSED
ON TO OTHERS.
LOVE IT AND SHARE IT WITH LIFE'S SISTERS AND
BROTHERS.

LIFE IS MORE THAN HEALTH & WEALTH, EVEN
THOUGH THAT'S GOOD.
LOVING LIFE THROUGHOUT OUR LIVES IS
SOMETHING THAT WE SHOULD.
LIFE IS MORE THAN BEING BORN TO DIE, IT WAS
MORE THAN JUST A PLAN.
IT IS TO LOVE LIFE AND VALUE LIFE OF THE
PRECIOUS WOMAN AND MAN.
LIFE IS A SUBJECT THAT'S TALKED ABOUT & A
LIFE RARELY LIVED.
IT IS THE TRUTH ABOUT THAT LOVE, MANY
SELDOM GIVE.
GENUINE LOVE IS THE ANSWER TO LIFE'S
BECKONING CALL.
SEEDS OF FAITH AND SEEDS OF LOVE IS A
CALLING FOR US ALL.
LIFE IS MORE THAN THE POSSESSIONS WE HAVE
THAT ONE DAY WE WILL
LEAVE BEHIND.
IT IS THE CHALLENGE TO CHANGE OUR
CHARACTER TO KEEP OTHERS
IN MIND.
LIFE IS MORE THAN STROLLING THROUGH THIS
EARTH AND MAKING SELFISH
PLANS.

LIFE IS CARING & SHARING WITHOUT
COMPARING IT IS THE LOVE AND WHOLE
DUTY OF MAN.

01.27.2020

ONE

THERE IS ONE ONE
THERE IS ONE TWO
THERE IS ONE GOD
THERE IS ONE YOU
THERE IS ONE THREE
THERE IS ONE FOUR
THERE IS ONE JESUS
THERE IS ONE DOOR
THERE IS ONE FIVE
THERE IS ONE SIX
THERE IS ONE STAY
THERE IS ONE EVICT
THERE IS ONE SEVEN
THERE IS ONE EIGHT
THERE IS ONE ON TIME
THERE IS ONE LATE
THERE IS ONE NINE
THERE IS ONE TEN
THERE IS ONE LOST
THERE IS ONE WIN
THERE IS ONE ELEVEN
THERE IS ONE TWELVE
THERE IS ONE HEAVEN
THERE IS ONE HELL

You May Think You Know

YOU MAY THINK BECAUSE YOU WENT TO
SEMINARY SCHOOL YOU HAVE LEARNED ALL
THERE IS TO KNOW
BUT IFYOU HAVE LEARNED THE WORD OF GOD
YOU WILL FIND IT'S NOT SO.
YOU MAY LIVE YOUR LIFE IN TRADITIONS
THINKING THAT'S ALL THERE IS
YOU MAY SEARCH FOR ALL KNOWLEDGE ONLY
TRADITION IS NOT GOD'S WILL.
THE ATHEIST SAYS THERE IS NO GOD THE
EVOLUTIONIST SAYS MAN EVOLVES.
BUT IN ALL THEIR SEARCHING AND DISBELIEF,
THERE OWN PROBLEMS ARE NOT SOLVED.
COMPLAINTS OF LIFE ARE MANY EXCUSES ON
THE OTHER HAND.
THEY CAUSE MANY TO FIND OUT IN LIFE HOW
MUCH THEY DON''T UNDERSTAND.
WE ARE ALL IN THE GARMENT OF DESTINY TIED
TOGETHER IN A HUDDLE.
WE ARE SEPERATED IN OUR HEARTS IS WHILE
THE WORLD SEEMS BEFUDDLED.
WHAT IS MAN BUT A VAPOR THAT HIS LIFE
FLASHES BEFORE HIM.

ONLY WHEN THAT VAPOR GROWS DISTANT IS
WHEN OUR LIVES GO DIM.
MANY LEARN THEIR PURPOSE IN LIFE OTHERS
ARE STILL CONFUSED SO FAR.
ONLY TO FIND OUT THROUGH THE OUTWARD
SEARCH THE INWARD MAN IS REALLY WHO
THEY ARE.
GO BEYOND YOURSELF AND REACH DEEP
WITHIN.
YOU WILL SEE YOUR TRADITIONS PASS AND A
NEW LIFE WILL BEGIN.
THINK OF THE ONE IN HEAVEN WHO IS
INTERCEDING FOR MAN.
THE ONLY WAY INTO HEAVEN IS TO CHOOSE HIS
SALVATION PLAN.
THE ATHEIST, THE BUDHIST, THE TEACHINGS OF
THEM ALL,
FAIL TO PROVE WHAT THEY ARE SEARCHING
FOR; WHAT THEY BELIEVE WILL FALL.
BELIEVE THE ONE WHO DIED FOR YOU, WENT TO
HELL AND TOOK THE KEYS.
WHO GAVE YOU THE KEYS OF VICTORY FOR
YOU TO BE AT EASE?
GO BEYOND THE COLOR BARRIER AND EXCUSES
IN THIS LAND.

GIVE YOUR LIFE TO A SAVIOR WHO DIED FOR
THE SINS OF EVERY MAN.

YOU MAY THINK BECAUSE YOU WENT TO
SEMINARY SCHOOL YOU HAVE LEARNED ALL
THERE IS TO KNOW, BUT IF YOU LEARN THE
WORD OF GOD, YOU WILL FIND IT'S NOT SO.

Where Is Your Witness

WHEN THE WORLD SEES YOU WHAT DO THEY SEE?
THE ENEMY IN THEM OR THE GREATER ONE IN THEE.
DOES THE WORLD SEE FAILURE OR DOES THE WORLD
SEE SUCCESS?
WILL THEY SEE YOU CURSED OR WILL THEY SEE YOU
BLESSED?
WHERE IS YOUR WITNESS TO THE WORLD OUTSIDE?
WILL THEY SEE A HYPOCRITE OR THE GREATER ONE
INSIDE?
WHEN THE WORLD SEES YOU WHAT DO THEY SAY?
WHERE IS YOUR WITNESS? WHY WOULD THEY
WOULD FOLLOW IF JESUS IS NOT THE WAY?
WHERE IS YOUR WITNESS? IS IT THE LIGHT OF THE
WORLD THEY SEE?
WILL THEY TASTE THE SALT IN YOU & FOLLOW FOR
ETERNITY?
WHERE IS YOUR WITNESS, DOES THE WORLD SEE IT
AT ALL?
AN EXAMPLE THE WORLD WILL SEE, IS WHEN WE
ANSWER OUR CALL.

3.31.2004

What Went Wrong

WHAT WENT WRONG WHEN FAMILIES STAYED TOGETHER AND WERE STRONG?

WHEN LOVE DEPARTED AND THE STAY WASN'T VERY LONG.

WHAT WENT WRONG WHEN DAD WAS THE BREAD WINNER?

WHEN MOM STAYED HOME, CLEANED, AND COOKED DINNER.

WHAT WENT WRONG WHEN FAMILIES LOVED ONE ANOTHER?

WHEN DAD LOVED MOM AND SISTER LOVED BROTHER.

WHAT WENT WRONG WHEN CHILDEN USED TO OBEY THE HOUSE RULES?

WHEN THEY WERE GIVEN EXTRA DUTIES BEFORE AND AFTER SCHOOL.

WHAT WENT WRONG WHEN MEN WORKED ALL DAY LONG

WHEN MEN WERE NOT WEAK, BUT ALWAYS STRONG

WHAT WENT WRONG WHEN RESPECT WAS UTMOST IN PLACE

WHEN WOMEN WERE QUEENS AND MEN WERE THEIR ACE.

WHAT WENT WRONG WHEN ALL SEEMS LOST AND NOTHING GAINED?

WHEN IT'S TIME FOR INCREASE AND NOT ADDED PAIN.

WHAT WENT WRONG THAT DIDN'T TAKE VERY LONG?

WHEN ALL IT TOOK WAS FOR MEN TO BE STRONG.

No Excuse for Failure

THERE IS NO EXCUSE FOR FAILURE AND I'M ONE THAT CAN TELL YOU BECAUSE I TRIED TO MAKE AS MANY AS POSSIBLE TO NO AVAIL.

NOW I DID NOT SAY THERE IS NO REASON FOR THE EXCUSES PEOPLE MAKE. NOW I KNOW THIS MAY BE A CONTROVERSAL STATEMENT, BUT THE TRUTH IS PEOPLE DON'T WANT TO FACE THE REALITY THAT THEY ARE WHERE THEY ARE BECAUSE OF THEIR OWN MIND SET.

TRULY SUCCESSFUL PEOPLE DO NOT AND CAN NOT MAKE EXCUSES IN ORDER TO SUCCEED. REMEMBER I SAID THERE ARE REASONS FOR FAILURE, BUT NO

EXCUSES FOR FAILURE.

IN THE BOOK OF ROMANS 1:19, THE WORD SAYS IN VERSE 19: "BECAUSE THAT WHICH MAY BE KNOWN OF GOD IS MANIFEST IN THEM; FOR GOD HATH SHEWED IT UNTO THEM. VERSE 20 SAYS FOR THE INVISIBLE THING OF HIM FROM THE CREATION OF THE WORLD ARE CLEARLY SEEN, BEING UNDERSTOOD BY THE THINGS THAT ARE MADE, EVEN HIS ETERNAL POWER

AND GODHEAD; SO THAT THEY ARE WITHOUT EXCUSE.

NOT EVERYONE THAT IS INVITED SHOWS UP TO PARTAKE OF THE BLESSINGS OF LIFE. IN THE BOOK OF LUKE, CHAPTER 14, VERSES16-27 TELL THE STORY OF PEOPLE MAKING EXCUSES.

DILIGENT PEOPLE AND PEOPLE OF PURPOSE DON'T MAKE EXCUSES

ONLY LAZY AND PURPOSELESS PEOPLE MAKE EXCUSES.

STILL, THERE IS NO JUSTIFIABLE REASON FOR THE EXCUSES THAT PEOPLE MAKE.

SOMETIMES, WE ALL NEED ENCOURAGEMENT ON OUR ROAD TO SUCCESS, HOWEVER WE NEED TO KNOW WHERE WE ARE GOING.

IT HAS BEEN SAID THAT IF YOU DON'T KNOW WHERE YOU ARE GOING ANY ROAD WILL TAKE YOU THERE.

THE ROAD OF EXCUSES IS THE ROAD TO FAILURE AND SOME PEOPLE FAIL FOR THE LACK OF KNOWLEDGE HOSEA 4-6.

IF YOU HAVE NOT TRIED ANYTHING YOU CAN'T FAIL AT ANYTHING.

ZERO ATTEMPTS EQUAL ZERO COMPLETIONS.

JESUS DIDN'T MAKE ANY EXCUSES WHEN HE WENT TO THE CROSS NEITHER DID, HE FAIL. REMEMBER THE CONFESSION THAT SAYS FOR DEATH HE [JESUS] HAS GIVEN ME LIFE, FOR SICKNESS HE HAS GIVEN ME HEALTH, FOR POVERTY HE HAS GIVEN ME WEALTH.

I THANK GOD FOR HAVING A MAN OF GOD THAT TEACHES THE WORD WITHOUT COMPROMISE SO THAT WE FULLY GRASP THE REVELATION THAT IS BEING TAUGHT AS HE MINISTERS THE WORD OF GOD.

ONCE WHILE I WAS PRAYING, I HEARD THIS IN MY SPIRIT: "FEAR AND LAZINESS IS THE FOUNDATION OF ALL CHRISTIANS FAILURE".

FEAR IS THE MOTHER OF LAZINESS AND LAZINESS IS THE FATHER OF FAILURE.

FOOLS DO LAST WHAT WISE MEN DO MATHEW CHAPTER 25 VERSES 1 THRU 13 TELL THE STORY OF TEN VIRGINS. FIVE WERE WISE AND FIVE WERE FOOLISH. THE FOOLISH DIDN'T USE WISDOM IN PREPARING FIRST, SO THEY MISSED OUT ON THE INVITATION TO THE WEDDING. THEY HAD ALL DAY LONG TO GET READY; THE WEDDING WASN'T UNTIL TWELVE MIDNIGHT. THE POINT HERE IS THERE WAS NO EXCUSE FOR

THAT MISSED OPPORTUNITY. EARLIER I MADE REFERENCE TO SOMETHING GOD SHOWED ME IN MY SPIRIT - THAT FEAR AND LAZINESS IS THE FOUNDATION OF ALL CHRISTIANS' FAILURE. FURTHER DOWN IN MATHEW CHAPTER 25, VERSES 14 THRU 30 TELL THE STORY OF TALENTS BEING GIVEN OUT ACCORDING TO THEIR INDIVIDUAL ABILITIES. THE FIVE AND TWO TALENTS WERE MULTIPLIED BUT THE PERSON WITH ONE TALENT MADE AN EXCUSE AND AS A RESULT EXPERIENCED NO INCREASE.

THE REASON HE GAVE WAS THAT HE WAS AFRAID. THAT WORD AFRAID IN GREEK MEANS TO BE FRIGHTENED OR ALARMED.

THE UNPROFITABLE, NON-INCREASING SERVANT WAS REFERED TO AS BEING LAZY AND AS A RESULT, THE LITTLE HE HAD WAS ALSO TAKEN AWAY FROM HIM AND GIVEN TO THE MAN WITH THE TEN TALENTS.

AS ONE SAYING GOES: USE IT OR LOSE IT.

EXCUSES TO ME ARE NO MORE THAN A DRESSED-UP LIE LEADING TO THE EXPOSER OF FAILURE.

NO MATTER WHAT REASONS WE USE TO EXPLAIN FAILURE, THERE ARE MORE THAN

ENOUGH EXAMPLES OF SUCCESSFUL PEOPLE TO NULLIFY ANY EXCUSES WE CAN MAKE CONCERNING FAILURE.

WHEN WE OPERATE IN THE LOVE OF GOD WE CAN NOT FAIL BECAUSE GOD IS LOVE AND LOVE NEVER FAILS. (1 Corinthians 13:8, 1 JOHN 4:8).

WE AS CHRISTIANS HAVE BEEN TAUGHT THAT THE PEOPLE PERISH FOR THE LACK OF A PROPHETIC VISION OR REVELATION.

VISION HELPS TO KEEP US FOCUSED, AND FOCUS WILL ASSIST US IN BEING DISCIPLINED. WE AS BELIEVERS MUST UNDERSTAND THAT WE ARE AGREEING WITH WHAT IS SAID WHEN WE ARE DOING WHAT IS SAID.

WHEN WE ARE TRULY PERSUING SUCCESS, THERE WILL BE NO EXCUSES.

ALL SUCCESS OR FAILURE IS BASED ON A DECISION. A DECISION IS BASED ON

AN INWARD OR AN OUTWARD DESIRE. AN OUTWARD DESIRE USUALLY SPELLS FAILURE. AN INWARD DESIRE USUALLY BREEDS SUCCESS.

FAILURE IS NOT WHAT OTHERS ARE NOT DOING FOR YOU BUT WHAT YOU ARE NOT DOING FOR YOURSELF. SUCCESS IS PERSONAL. THEREFORE, GET CONFRONTATIONAL! CONFRONT

YOUR ENEMY CALLED FAILURE.

WANTING TO PLEASE EVERYBODY IS NOT AS BAD AS NOT PLEASING ANYBODY AND BEING DISSAPPOINTED.

TO SUCCEED IN LIFE, WE MUST LEARN TO ACCEPT THAT GOD HASPROVEN METHODS INSTEAD OF TRYING TO COME UP WITH TIME-WASTING EXPERIMENTS.

NOT THAT WE CAN'T BE CREATIVE, BUT MOST OF THE TIME WE WASTE IS TIME TRYING TO REINVENT WHAT ALREADY EXISTS.

SUCCESS IS LIKE BLOOD AND WATER: BOTH ARE NEEDED TO SUSTAIN LIFE. FAILURE IS LIKE ALCOHOL" DESIGNED TO EAT AWAY AT SUCCESS IN LIFE WHILE WE TEND TO IGNORE ITS POTENTIAL.

WE MUST CHOOSE OUR OWN DESTINY BECAUSE NO ONE ELSE CAN CHOOSE IT FOR US.

LIFE IS LIKE A MAP OUTLINED WITH DIFFERENT DESTINATIONS AND WHATEVER WE DECIDE, FAILURE OR SUCCESS, WILL BE CARRIED OUT.

I HAVE LEARNED FROM MY MAN OF GOD, PASTOR CREFLO A. DOLLAR JR., THAT DECISIONS ARE THE OPEN DOOR TO REALITY.

THE REALITY AND TRUTH IS THAT THERE IS NO EXCUSE FOR FAILURE.

WE HAVE ANSWERS WAITING IN THE PRESENCE OF GOD BUT WE MUST GET INTO HIS PRESENCE TO RECEIVE THOSE ANSWERS.

SUCCESS IS A SUBJECT MOSTLY DECUSSED AND RARELY LIVED.

FAILURE IS A SUBJECT MOSTLY DECUSSED AND MOSTLY LIVED.

LIFE IS A GIFT AND A GIFT IS FREE TO THE RECIEVER FROM THE GIVER OF LIFE.

SUCCESS IS AT THE EXPENSE OF THE INDIVIDUAL'S EFFORT.

LIFE IS A SUBJECT WITH AN ENDLESS DECUSSION; SOARE EXCUSES AND THEY ARE ENDLESS IN LIFE.

ANYONE LOOKING FOR SOMEONE TO UNDERSTAND THEIR BAD SITUATION IS ASKING FOR COMFORT IN THAT SITUATION.

TOTAL FAILURE IN LIFE IS THE RESULT OF SOME SIN IN A PERSON'S LIFE BECAUSE FAILURE IS NOT OF GOD.

GIVING UP IS THE ENDLESS ROAD TO FAILURE AND THERE IS NOTHING ELSE ON THE AGENDA.

NEGATIVE OR POSITIVE WORDS CARRY THE ABILITY TO BRING ITSELF TO PASS.

SO, SPEAK SUCCESS, MEDITATE ON SUCCESS, THINK SUCCESS, ACT SUCCESS, ETC.

BLAMING SOMEONE ELSE FOR YOUR FAILURE IS A LIE ON YOUR PART.

THE BIBLE SAYS IN PROVERBS 6:6-8 "GO TO THE ANT THOU SLUGGARD CONSIDER HER WAYS AND BE WISE.

7 WHICH HAVING NO GUIDE, OVERSEER OR RULER, 8 PROVIDETH HER

MEAT IN THE SUMMER, AND GATHERETH HER FOOD IN THE HARVEST."

EVEN THE EXAMPLES OF ANTS WILL PREVENT FAILURE WHEN YOU CONSIDER HOW DILIGENTLY THEY ARE AT WORKING IN THE SUMMER AND HAVE ENOUGH FOOD TO LAST THROUGH THE WINTER.

ANTS DO NOT BORROW, BEG, STEAL OR TAKE OUT A LOAN TO CARRY THEM THROUGH THE NEXT SEASON.

THEY ARE NOT LAZY. THEY WORK AND EARN THEIR KEEP.

FEAR AND LAZINESS IS THE FOUNDATION OF ALL CHRISTIANS' FAILURE.

THEREFORE, THERE IS NO EXCUSE FOR FAILURE. FAILURE IS A WAY OF THINKING AND THINKING MAKES IT SO.

AS A MAN THINKS, IN HIS HEART, SO IS HE, AS HE THINKS ACCORDING TO PROVERBS 23:7AND MATTHEW 15: 18-19. AND 12: 34-35

WE MUST NOT BE CONFORMED TO THIS WORLD'S SYSTEM, BUT BE TRANSFORMED BY THE RENEWING OF OUR MIND WHICH WE RENEW BY THE WORD OF GOD.

I REMEMBER A LITTLE SAYING WHEN I WAS IN SALES THAT GOES LIKE THIS:

KIND HEARTS ARE THE GARDEN.

KIND THOUGHTS ARE THE ROOTS.

KIND WORDS ARE THE BLOSSOM.

KIND DEEDS ARE THE FRUITS.

WORDS ARE LIKE MAGNETS IN THAT THEY NEVER LOSE THEIR SUBSTANCE. LIKEWISE, FAILURE NEVER LOSES ITS MAGNITISM BECAUSE IT IS OF THE DEVIL.

THE BIBLE SAYS IN PROVERB 29: 18THAT WITHOUT A REDEMPTIVE REVELATION THE PEOPLE PERISH[AMP]

OUR OBEDIENCE TO GOD'S WORD IS AT HIS EXPENSE

OUR DISOBEDIENCE TO HIS WORD IS AT OUR EXPENSE

THERE IS NO EXCUSE FOR FAILURE EVEN IF YOU CAN EXPLAIN WHY SOMETHING DID NOT WORK IT STILL CAN NOT JUSTIFY FAILURE.

OBEDIENCE IS THE PROOF THAT VERIFIES OUR BELIEF.

LIVING RIGHT OR LIVING WRONG, BOTH WILL BRING RESULTS.

WE MUST HAVE DETERNMINATION LIKE THE EAGLE.

THE EAGLE SOARS HIGH ABOVE THE SITUATION AND LOOKS DOWN ON WHAT HE SOARS ABOVE.

WE MUST BELIEVE THE WORD OF GOD CONCERNING OUR LIVES TO ITS FULL POTENTIAL.

ACCORDING TO II TIMOTHY 1:7, GOD HAS NOT GIVEN US THE SPIRIT OF FEAR BUT OF POWER, LOVE AND A SOUND MIND.

ACCORDING TO LUKE 10:19 "BEHOLD, I GIVE YOU POWER TO TREAD ON SERPENTS, SCORPIONS, AND OVER ALL THE POWER [ABILITY] OF THE ENEMY AND NOTHING SHALL BY ANY MEANS HURT YOU [ME].

IGNORING WHAT YOU KNOW IS CALLED NEGLECT AND WHAT YOU FAIL TO DEAL WITH WILL BE RESPONSIBLE FOR YOUR DOWNFALL.

DON'T LET FEAR ROB YOU OF YOUR ALREADY GOD-GIVEN VICTORY.

WE MUST LET THE LOVE OF GOD BE SHED ABROAD IN OUR HEARTS BY THE HOLY GHOST ACCORDING TO ROMANS 5:5 AND PHILIPPIANS 2:5 WHICH SAYS, "LET THIS MIND BE IN YOU WHICH WAS ALSO IN CHRIST JESUS."

FOLLOWING IN THE FOOTSTEPS OF JESUS IS THE PATHWAY TO SUCCESS, AND THERE IS NO FAILURE IN HIM.

WE AS CHRISTIANS MUST NOT BECOME FUGITIVES TO OUR RESPONSIBILITY.

EFFORT WITHOUT FAITH IS FRUITLESS AND HOWEVER IT MAY GLITTER IS STILL BARREN OF ALL PERMANENT GOOD.

FAILURE IS A BY-PRODUCT OF LAZINESS AND LAZINESS IS A BY PRODUCT OF FEAR. GOD MADE US FREE MORAL AGENTS THEREFORE WE ARE FREE TO CHOOSE WHATEVER LIFE OR LIFESTYLE WE WANT.

GOD HAS NOTHING TO DO WITH OUR FAILURE OR REALLY OUR SUCCESS BECAUSE HE DOES

NOT MAKE EITHER CHOICE FOR US. WE MUST CHOOSE LIFE OR DEATH, BLESSING OR CURSING, BECAUSE WE HAVE BEEN MADE FREE MORAL AGENTS BY GOD HIMSELF.

IT IS UP TO US TO BE WORD-COMPLIANT. IT MUST BE OUR UNDERSTANDING THAT MAKES THE DIFFERENCE IN OUR LIVES.

THE BIBLE SAYS IN II TIMOTHY 2:15 TO STUDY TO SHOW THYSELF APPROVED UNTO GOD A WORKMAN THAT NEEDETH NOT TO BE ASHAMED, RIGHTLY DIVIDING THE WORD OF TRUTH.

KNOW THE TRUTH- JOHN 8:32. DESIRE THE TRUTH: PSALM 51:6.

WALK IN TRUTH- PSALM 26:3 SPEAK THE TRUTH- PROVERBS 8:7.

REJOICE IN TRUTH-1 CORINTHIANS 13:6 LIPS OF THUTH –PROVERBS 12:19

BUY THE TRUTH-PROVERBS 23:23. SCRIPTURE OF TRUTH-DANIEL 10:21

 GOD OF TRUTH-DEUTERONOMY 32:4. SPIRIT OF TRUTH – 1 JOHN 4:6.

WITNESS OF TRUTH- JOHN 18:37 DO THE TRUTH- JOHN 3:21.

ANOTHER REASON THAT THERE IS NO EXCUSE FOR FAILURE IS THAT GOD IS NOT A MAN THAT HE SHOULD LIE; NEITHER THE SON OF MAN, THAT HE SHOULD REPENT. HATH HE SAID, AND SHALL HE NOT DO IT? OR HATH HE SPOKEN AND SHALL HE NOT MAKE IT GOOD? (NUMBER 23:19). GOD IS A COVENANT-KEEPING GOD; HE SAID MY COVENANT WILL I NOT BREAK NOR ALTER THE THING THAT IS GONE OUT OF MY LIPS. [PSALMS 89:34]. GOD HAS A COVENANT OF PROMISE WITH THOSE THAT BELIEVE AND RECEIVE THE COVENANT. WE MUST NOT EXPECT TO RECEIVE SOMETHING THAT WE DON'T HAVE A RIGHT TO EXPECT, SUCH AS WANTING GOD TO DO HIS PART WITHOUT US DOING OUR PART WHICH IS TO BELIEVE.

REMEMBER GOD IS NOT UNRIGHTEOUS TO FORGET OUR WORK AND LABOR OF LOVE THAT WE HAVE SHOWN TOWARD HIS NAME, IN THAT WE HAVE MINISTERED TO THE SAINTS, AND DO MINISTER, ACCORDING TO

HEBREWS 6:10. WE AS BELIEVERS HAVE A WAY OF ESCAPE THROUGH THE WORD OF GOD. ACCORDING TO 1 CORINTHIANS 10:13. JESUS SAW OUR DELIVERANCE THROUGH HIS OBEDIENCE

TO THE FATHER, WHEN HE SAID NOT MY WILL BUT THY WILL BE DONE.

IT HAS ALWAYS BEEN THE FATHER'S WILL TO SEE HIS CHILDREN FREE FROM ALL TYPES OF BONDAGE, INCLUDING POVERTY.

WE AS BELIEVERS MUST BEGIN TO TRUST GOD WITH ALL OUR HEARTS AND LEAN NOT TO OUR OWN UNDERSTANDING AND ACKNOWLEDGE HIM IN ALL OUR WAYS AND HE WILL DIRECT OUR PATH. (PROVERBS 3:5-6) POVERTY IS A SPIRITUAL DISEASE BEING POOR IS NOT OF GOD. BEING IN WANT MAKES YOU DO EVIL THINGS, BUT THERE IS HOPE BECAUSE THERE IS GOD. AND HIS LOVE AND DESIRE IS FOR YOU TO MAKE IT.

AS I HAVE SAID BEFORE, FAILURE IS NOT OF GOD BUT OF THE DEVIL.

LET US HOLD FAST OUR PROFESSION OR CONFESSION OF FAITH [HEBREWS 4:14]. MAN FAILS GOD BUT GOD NEVER FAILS MAN; NEITHER DID JESUS FAIL GOD NOR MAN.

THE BIBLE CONSISTS OF 66 BOOKS OF WHAT, HOW, WHERE, WHEN, AND WHY THINGS HAPPEN SO THAT THERE IS NO LEGITIMATE EXCUSE FOR FAILURE. THE HABITS OF POOR PEOPLE KEEP

THEM POOR, BUT THE HABITS OF THE DILIGENT SHALL CAUSE THEM TO BE MADE FAT OR RICH.

JESUS SAID I CAME THAT YOU MAY HAVE LIFE AND HAVE IT MORE ABUNDANTLY [JOHN 10:10]. JESUS SAID I BECAME POOR THAT YOU THROUGH MY POVERTY MIGHT BE MADE RICH. [II COR.8:9].

II CORINTHIANS 9:8 SAYS THAT GOD IS ABLE TO MAKE ALL GRACE ABOUND TOWARDS US. THAT WE, HAVING ALL SUFFICIENCY IN ALL THINGS, MAY ABOUND TO EVERY GOOD WORK AS IT IS WRITTEN, HE HATH DISPERSED ABROAD; HE HATH GIVEN TO THE POOR AND HIS RIGHTEOUSNESS REMAINETH FOREVER.

TRUE PROSPERITY IS THE DEMONSTRATION OF HOLY AND RIGHTEOUS LIVING, BY BELIEVING IN THE WORD OF GOD.

THE ABOVE SCRIPTURES VOID ALL EXCUSES AND CANCEL ALL JUSTIFICATION FOR FAILURE.

TO AVOID FAILURE, AVOID EXCUSES AND BECOME SUCCESSFUL IN LIFE.

ACCORDING TO MATTHEW 11:5, JOHN SENT TWO OF HIS DISCIPLES TO ASK JESUS WAS HE THE ONE OR SHOULD HE LOOK FOR SOMEONE ELSE TO GET HIM OUT OF PRISON THERE WAS NO

REASON FOR JOHN TO DOUBT JESUS OR ASK WAS THERE ANOTHER TO GET HIM OUT OF JAIL BECAUSE HE KNEW BETTER.

CHRISTIANS ARE NOT IN AS MUCH ERROR IN THEIR SPEAKING AS IN THEIR DOING, FOR IN THEIR ACTIONS OR DOINGS, THEY EXPRESS MORE OF WHAT THEY THINK THAN WHAT THEY SPEAK.

THE BIBLE SAYS IN 1 JOHN 2:20 THAT WE HAVE AN UNCTION OR AN ANOINTING FROM THE HOLY ONE, AND WE KNOW ALL THINGS.

WHEN WE ABIDE IN THE TRUTH, WE ABIDE IN HIM. AND HIS WORD IS TRUTH (JOHN 17:17)

OUR VERY EXISTENCE DEPENDS ON HIS PRESENCE IN OUR LIVES AT ALL TIMES. WE SHOULD ALWAYS WANT GOD'S BEST FOR OUR LIVES AND NOT SETTLE FOR MEDIOCRITY.

WE AS BELIEVERS SHOULD NOT BE BARELY GETTING ALONG IN A WORLD OF JOY AND PLENTY BECAUSE GOD MADE HIS PROMISES KNOWN AND AVAILABLE. THEREFORE, WE HAVE NO EXCUSE. THE BIBLE SAYS IN GALATIANS 3:11 THAT IT IS EVIDENT: FOR, THE JUST SHALL LIVE BY FAITH. THE RESULTS OF FAITH IS CALLED EVIDENCE. THE EVIDENCE OF FAITH IS CALLED

RESULTS. WE HAVE ACCESS INTO THE SPIRIT REALM BY SPEAKING BOLDLY THE FAITH ON THE INSIDE OF US. REVELATION KNOWLEDGE IS THE SHIELD AND FREEDOM FROM ALL TYPES OF BONDAGE.

FEAR IS AT THE HEAD OF ALL FAILURE, LIKE LOVE IS AT THE HEAD OF ALL SUCCESS AND REALIZING THIS TRUTH MEANS THERE IS NO EXCUSE FOR FAILURE. PROCRASTINATION IS THE THIEF OF TIME AND TIME WILL RUN OUT. THE CLOCK DIDN'T START TIME, GOD DID. WHAT WE DO FOR CHRIST WILL LAST. AND, AS LONG WE LAST WHILE WE ARE DOING FOR CHRIST.

THERE IS NO CONCLUSION TO LIFE SINCE THERE IS LIFE AFTER DEATH AND WE MUST DECIDE WHERE WE WANT TO SPEND THE REST OF OUR LIVES: IN HEAVEN OR IN HELL. THE CHOICE IS NOT ONLY HERE ON EARTH, BUT THE TIME IS NOW ON EARTH. YOU MUST MAKE THAT DECISION BECAUSE THE LIFE YOU HAVE AFTER DEATH IS BASED ON THE DECISION YOU WILL HAVE MADE ON EARTH.

SINCE ALL ANSWERS ARE WITHIN THE WORD OF GOD, W HAT QUESTION CAN YOU ASK THAT CAN'T BE ANSWERED THERE? NONE.

TO SAY THAT IT IS NOT MEANT FOR EVERYBODY TO BE PROSPEROUS IS TO SAY THAT GOD IS A RESPECTOR OF PERSON SAND WE KNOW THAT IS NOT THE TRUTH ACCORDING TO THE WORD OF GOD IN ROMANS 2:11.

THE BLIND SEE, THE DEAF HEAR, THE LAME WALK, THE DEAD ARE RAISED UP, THE POOR HAVE THE GOSPEL OR GOOD NEWS PREACHED TO THEM, AND THE SICK ARE MADE WELL. SO, TELL ME, WHERE IS THE EXCUSE FOR FAILURE?

THE BIBLE SAYS THAT WISDOM IS THE PRINCIPAL THING AND IN ALL THY GETTING, GET UNDERSTANDING. GET UNDERSTANDING OF THE TRUTH THAT WISDOM IS THE PRINCIPAL THING OR THE MAIN INGREDIENT TO DISCERNMENT. IN THIS LIFE YOU WILL EITHER SPEAK, THINK OR ACT WORDS BUT WORDS WILL BE A PART OF YOUR LIFE. YOU CAN THINK WRONG WORDS, ACT WRONG WORDS, OR SPEAK WRONG WORDS AND THERE IS NO AVOIDING IT. EVEN WHILE READING THIS YOU ARE PROBALLY THINKING ABOUT WHAT I'M SAYING OR RESPONDING IN A CERTAIN WAY.

SINCE GOD MADE US FREE MORAL AGENTS, CHOOSING RIGHT OR WRONG WORDS IS AN ACT

OF OUR FREE WHICH LEAVES US WITHOUT EXCUSE FOR OUR OUTCOMES.

IT IS NOT WRONG TO BE DIFFERENT, BUT IT IS WRONG TO BE INDIFFERENT.

WHEN PEOPLE CARE IT MAKES A DIFFERENCE, WHEN THEY DON'T IT DOES AS WELL.

SOMETIMES PEOPLE MAKE EXCUSES BY USING PHRASES SUCH AS "BETTER LATE THAN NEVER, WHICH IS OFTEN SAID TO MEAN "AT LEAST I SHOWED UP". THIS IS AN EXCUSE IN PLACE OF AN APOLOGY.

OTHER SAYINGS LIKE YOU'D BETTER BE GLAD THAT I'M DOING THIS FOR YOU

INSTEAD OF "I'M GLAD TO BE DOING THIS FOR YOU."

WE MUST RECOGNIZE THAT IT ONLY MATTERS WHEN IT COMES FROM THE HEART BECAUSE THE HEART OF THE MATTER IS IN THE HEART.

EXCUSES CAN NOT BE JUSTIFIED WHEN THERE WAS A CHOICE. EXCUSES ARE DESIGNED TO CRIPPLE OUR FORWARD PROGRESS AND HOLD US IN CONTEMPT FOR SPEAKING THE WORD OF GOD. HOWEVER, THE WORD OF GOD SAYS IN HEBREWS 12:1 THAT WE ARE SURROUNDED BY A CLOUD OF WITNESSES AND WE ARE TO LAY

ASIDE EVERY WEIGHT AND SIN WHICH EASILY BESET US AND LET US RUN WITH PATIENCE{PERSEVERANCE} THE RACE THAT IS SET BEFORE US.

WE MUST USE OUR FAITH AND LOVE TO ACTIVATE THAT SLEEPING GIANT IN US CALLED ABILITY.

CONSISTENCY IS A FAITH SUPPORTER OF A GUARNTEED BREAKTHROUGH.

GOD WILL KEEP HIS WORD BECAUSE HE [GOD] CAN NOT LIE. (NUMBERS 23:19)

GOD WILL HASTEN HIS WORD TO PERFORM IT ACCORDING JER 1:12.

REMEMBER GOD IS A COVENANT-KEEPING GOD PSALM 89:34

WE AS BELIEVERS MUST NOT ENVY THE SUCCESS OF FOOLS BECAUSE WE

UNDERSTAND THEIR OUTCOME (PSALM 73:3,17)

IT IS CONSIDERED A NATURAL THING FOR PEOPLE TO THINK NEGATIVELY AT FIRST AND THEN BE TRAINED TO THINK POSITIVE BECAUSE OF THE SIN NATURE OF MAN.

CONSIDERING THAT KNOWLEDGE IS SO RELEVENT AND EASILY AVAILABLE. IT AIDS IN THE TRUTH THAT THERE IS NO EXCUSE FOR

FAILURE. FAILURE IS OFTEN TIMES DUE TO IMPROPER PLANNING.

IF IT IS NOT IN THE WORD OF GOD, THEN IT SHOULD NOT BE IN YOUR LIFE.

THE FRUIT OF THE SPIRIT IS LOVE, JOY, PEACE, LONGSUFFERING, GENTLENESS, GOODNESS, FAITH, MEEKNESS, ANDTEMPERANCE: AGAINST SUCH THERE IS NO LAW. HATRED ACTIVATES FAILURE WHILE LOVE ACTIVATES SUCCESS, BECAUSE LOVE NEVER FAILS.

PROCRASTINATION

PROCRASTINATION IS THE THIEF OF TIME THAT CANNOT BE RETRIEVED BECAUSE TIME DOES NOT STAND STILL. IT KEEPS MOVING UNTIL ETERNITY STOPS IT.

IT IS AN ACT OF DELAYING SOMETHING THAT SHOULD BE DONE NOW, AND UNFORTUNATELY MOST PEOPLE FALL INTO THE TRAP OF "I'LL DO IT LATER SYNDROME". TO PROCRASTINATE IS TO DELAY PRESENT PROGRESS.

TO BE A PROCRASTINATOR IS LIKE PROMISING YOURSELF THAT YOU HAVE ALL THE TIME IN THE WORLD TO DO WHAT YOU HAVE PUT OFF UNTIL LATER.

I HAVE FOUND THAT LATER, MOST TIMES, TURNS INTO NEVER, ONE MORE TIME BECOMES ONE MORE TIME WHICH LEADS TO NEVER. LAZINESS, INDECISIVENESS, I GOT TIME, I'LL DO IT LATER, WHAT'S THE HURRY: THESE SAYINGS ARE TIED TO PROCRASTINATION. I'M WRITING THIS BECAUSE I HEARD MY PASTOR TEACH ON THIS AND I KNEW THAT I WAS A GUILTY PARTY. AS A RESULT OF HIS MESSAGE, I HAVE MADE A

DECISION TO CHANGE THIS BAD HABIT OF PUTTING OFF THE NOW FOR LATER.
THE BIBLE SAYS NOW IS THE ACCEPTABLE TIME, NOW IS THE DAY OF SALVATION, 2COR 6:2; NOT LATER. PROCRASTINATION OF SALVATION HAS COST SOME HEAVENS MANSION THAT WAS RESERVED FOR THEM.
NOW FAITH IS THE SUBSTANCE OF THINGS HOPED FOR AND THE EVIDENCE OF THINGS NOT SEEN. (HEBREWS 11:1)
LEARNING FROM JESUS AND FOLLOWING HIS EXAMPLE, IS TO UNDERSTAND THAT NOTHING GETS DONE WITHOUT SOME ACTION. FAITH WITHOUT WORKS IS DEAD. WE WERE MEANT TO BE ALL THAT WE ARE IN CHRIST JESUS AND OUR EXISTENCE WAS IN HIM BEFORE WE KNEW IT (JEREMIAH 1:5, ISAIAH 49:1, EXODUS 33:12) WE MUST UNDERSTAND THE SPIRIT BEHIND BOTH WRONG & RIGHT FOCUS. LOOKING THROUGH THE LENS OF TRADITION, WHICH MAKES THE WORD OF GOD OF NONE EFFECT, IS THE WRONG FOCUS. LIKEWISE SEEING THE WORD THROUGH THE LENS OF GRACE BRING US TO THE SPIRIT OF RIGHT FOCUS.

SPIRITUALLY SPEAKING, WE CAN'T HAVE A "HEART BYPASS" BECAUSE IT IS THE SOIL WHERE THE SEED OF THE WORD IS SOWN. THERE WERE FOUR GROUNDS (OR HEARTS) THAT THE SEED WAS SOWN INTO BUT ONLY ONE PRODUCED. IF IT HAD BEEN "BYPASSED" OR NOT SOWN, THERE WOULD NOT HAVE BEEN A HARVEST. IF NO ONE ELSE, BELIEVERS SHOULD BE GRATEFUL, SPIRITUAL SPEAKING UNGRATEFULNESS IS THE BEGINNING OF POVERTY. I BELIEVE TO SOME DEGREE THAT POVERTY IS THE FRUIT OF IGNORANCE & IGNORANCE IS THE ROOT OF MISFORTUNE. OUR DESIRE TO DO IT OUR WAY SET THE FUTURE FOR THE OUTCOME IN OUR LIVES. THE CHRISTIANS WALK & WAY SHOULD NOT BE BURGER KING OR FRANK SINATRA METHOD, THIS IS NOT A I DID IT MY WAY GOSPEL AND WE MUST CONCEDE TO THE GOSPEL OF GRACE, BECAUSE HIS GRACE IS ENOUGH FOR US.

Voice of God

GOD'S VOICE IS HIS INSTRUCTION. GOD'S VOICE IS HIS DIRECTION. GOD'S VOICE IS HIS CORRECTION. GOD'S VOICE IS HIS PROTECTION. GOD CREATED MAN AND UNDERSTANDS MAN. THEREFORE, HE DOESN'T NEED AN INTERPRETER TO KNOW THE LANGUAGE OF MAN.

WE WILL NEVER BE ENOUGH IN AND OF OURSELVES BUT JESUS IS ENOUGH FOR US ALL THE TIME.

HOW MUCH TIME HAVE YOU GIVEN AWAY TO THE THINGS THAT YOU CAN'T HELP AND WHAT IS THE ESTIMATED VALUE OF THAT WASTED TIME?

WE MUST ADHERE TO OUR RESPONSIBILITY KNOWING THAT THE GREATEST THING IN LIFE AND ABOUT LIFE IS BEING BORN AGAIN AND THE SECOND GREATEST THING IN LIFE IS RENEWING THE MIND. (ROMANS 10:9,10 ROMANS 12:2)

WE ALL ARE WITNESSES WHETHER VOLUNTARILY OR INVOLUNTARILY BECAUSE IT IS NOT GOD'S WILL FOR YOU TO LEAVE HIM OUT OF YOUR LIFE.

LET THE WORD BE AND HAVE THE FINAL WORD
OR SAY IN YOUR LIFE.

LORD, HELP US TO FIND HELP IN HELPLESS
SITUATIONS, LOVE IN A LOVELESS SITUATIONS,
CARE IN A CARELESS SITUATIONS, HOPE IN A
HOPELESS SITUATIONS, JOY IN A JOYLESS
SITUATIONS, AND FAITH IN A FAITHLESS
SITUATIONS.

WE AS BELIEVERS CAN'T AFFORD TO
COMPROMISE OUR SPIRITUAL MORALS IN
EXCHANGE FOR A POLITICAL OR FINANCIAL
FAVOR.

WE MUST HAVE CONVICTION WITHOUT
COMPROMISE AND ALSO UNDERSTAND THAT
WHEN WE COMPROMISE, OUR CONVICTION IS
NULLIFIED

THERE IS A DIFFERENCE BETWEEN
COMPROMISE AND ADJUSTING TO WHAT IS THE
WISEST THING TO DO AT THE TIME.

STANDARDS CARRY CONVICTIONS ABOUT WHAT
WE TRULY BELIEVE CONCERNING THE WORD OF
GOD AND THAT, WITHOUT COMPROMISING OUR
BELIEF.

AS WE RENEW OUR MIND BY THE WORD OF GOD
AND SEEK THE PURPOSE OF GOD FOR OUR

LIVES, WE CAN OBTAIN THE WISDOM NEEDED BY LEARNING FROM THE MASTER AND LEADING BY EXAMPLE.

NOTHING IN THIS LIFE GETS DONE WITHOUT SOME FORM OF ACTION AND THAT BY THE FAITH OF GOD. REMEMBER FAITH WITHOUT WORKS IS DEAD.

GRACE IS THE PERSON WITH THE PRODUCT AND FAITH IS THE PERSON THAT RECEIVES THAT PRODUCT. WE AS BELIEVERS WERE MEANT TO BE ALL THAT WE CAN BE IN CHRIST.

IF JESUS IS NOT IN YOUR LIFE, THEN HE IS THE ONLY WAY OUT OF THE LIFE THAT YOU'RE IN. WE SHOULD EXAMINE THE LOGIC BEHIND OUR THINKING BECAUSE NOTHING JUST HAPPENS. OUR BELIEF IS THE WEAVER OF OUR ACCOMPLISHMENTS.

ONE OF THE GREATEST THINGS THAT WE CAN KNOW IS THAT GOD LOVES US. REMEMBER THAT A WATERED-DOWN VERSION OF THE WORD OF GOD HAS NO REAL BENEFIT BECAUSE IT IS DILUTED AND VOIDED OF ITS POTENTIAL.

YOUR SPIRIT IS THE REAL YOU AND THE SOUL IS THE MIND, WILL AND EMOTIONS OF YOU AND THE BODY IS THE HOUSE OF THE OTHER TWO.

GOD IS TRUE AND SENT HIS SON TO DIE FOR YOU AND THE HOLY SPIRIT TO LEAD AND GUIDE YOU INTO ALL TRUTH. THEREFORE, LIFE HAS BEEN GIVEN AND DIRECTIONS HAVE BEEN PROVIDED, LEAVING US WITH NO EXCUSE FOR FAILURE. WE HAVE THE WORD AS EVIDENCE THAT ALL MANKIND WAS CREATED IN THE IMAGE AND LIKENESS OF THE CREATOR [GOD] HIMSELF. WE KNOW THAT CHANGE ISN'T A 360 DEGREE TURN BUT A 180 DEGREE TURN AND THIS IS TRUTH. IF YOU ARE INTIMIDATED BY THE TRUTH THEN THAT MEANS YOU NEED TO GROW UP.

IF WE WANT TO CHANGE OUR LIVES, WE MUST CHANGE OUR WAY OF THINKING AND BE AVAILABLE TO BE CORRECTED BY THE QUALIFIED WORD OF GOD.

LET US WRITE THE VISION AND MAKE IT PLAIN AND SIMPLE SIMPLY, WE WON'T COMPROMISE THE WORD OF GOD IN OUR LIVES.

OUR LOVE MAY BE EXPRESSED IN WORDS BUT IT MUST BE DEMONSTRATED IN ACTION.

WE NEED TO STOP BEING PART TIME CHRISTIANS, LOOKING FOR FULL TIME

BENEFITS. WE ARE SLOWLY AND SURELY
BECOMING WHAT WE'RE GOING TO BE.
LOVE IS THE ESSENCE AND MORAL QUALITIES
OF GOD HIMSELF AND WE AS BELIEVERS
SHOULD EXPRESS THOSE QUALITIES IN OUR
LOVE WALK.
I WILL PRACTICE GIVING THANKS EVERYDAY
FOR ALL THAT GOD HAS DONE FOR ME, MY
FAMILY AND OTHERS, AND FOR HIS LOVE, HIS
MERCY AND GRACE.
OUR SUCCESS IS MOVING FORWARD IN GOD'S
WORD, BUT NOT WITHOUT OPPOSITION,
INTERRUPTIONS, AND UNDERSTANDING THAT
FAILURE IS ONLY PERMANENT IF YOU NEVER
START.
LET YOUR LIFE BECOME THE PROOF THAT YOU
BELIEVE THE WORD OF GOD BECAUSE MANY
PEOPLE SAY THEY BELIEVE BUT THEN
QUESTION THE VALIDITY OF TRUTH. WE
SHOULD NEVER COMPROMISE THE TRUTH.
THE WORLD IS FULL OF CRITICISM CONCERNING
SUCCESS OF CHRISTIANS, BUT IF LIFE WAS
WITHOUT PERSECUTION, PREPARATION WOULD
BE UNNECESSARY.

THE WORD OF GOD IS THE MAJOR FACTOR IN
CONTROLLING POSITIVE EMOTIONS THAT HELP
MOVE US IN THE RIGHT DIRECTION.

WHEN IT COMES TO THE WORD, GIVING ALL IS
SIMPLY BEING SOLD OUT TO JESUS AND HIS
WORD.

WISDOM IS THE PRINCIPAL THING, LOVE IS THE
MAIN THING, AND PEACE OF MIND IS THE
ULTIMATE THING. WE WERE GUILTY BY THE SIN
NATURE OF ADAM BUT FOUND INNOCENT AND
FORGIVEN BY THE SUPREME JUDGE GOD WHO
SITS ON THE THRONE AND NOT THE BENCH.
WHEN WE ACCEPTED CHRIST. AND WE SHOULD
STICK WITH BIBLICAL BASICS.

IT IS POSSIBLE TO CHANGE YOUR
CIRCUMSTANCES AND STILL BE UNWILLING TO
CHANGE YOURSELF, THEREFORE REMAINING
THE SAME PERSON. A THIEF IN A SHACK CAN
MOVE TO A MANSION BUT STILL BE A THIEF. A
LOCATION CHANGE IS NOT A CHANGE OF
CHARACTER. AS A MAN THINK, IN HIS HEART SO
IS HE. AND OUT OF THAT SAME HEART HE SAYS
WHAT HE THINKS. EXCUSES ARE NOT IN THE
COVENANT OF GOD.

REMEMBER ONE OF POVERTY'S BIGGEST
SUPPORTER'S IS EXCUSES; THE WAY CREDIT
SUPPORTS INFLATION.WE MUST NOT LET FEAR
SET UP RESIDENCE IN OUR MIND, BUT RATHER
BY FAITH. WE MUST WRITE THE VISION ON OUR
HEARTS AND MIND BEFORE WE WRITE IT ON
PAPER. THE TONGUE IS THE PEN OF A READY
WRITER, WRITING ON OUR HEARTS WITH
WORDS.

MOVING FORWARD IN LIFE IS GETTING PAST
HURT AND PAIN AND THIS SOMETIMES
REQUIRES INVENTORY OF OUR FOCUS.
SELF-RIGHTEOUSNESS IS COMPARING THE DO'S
& DON'T'S OF WORDS AND ACTIONS.
WE MUST RELY TOTALLY ON OUR CREATOR. YOU
CAN'T GO TO THE FORD MOTOR PLANT AND
FIND A CHEVROLET COMING OFF THE ASSEMBLY
LINE.

THERE IS NOTHING YOU KNOW THAT HAS NOT
BEEN KNOWN BEFORE YOU KNEW IT.
HOW WILL YOU KNOW THAT IT DOESN'T WORK,
IF IT DOESN'T FAIL?
I PRACTICE BY FAITH EVERYDAY CONFESSING
THAT I AM A PSALM 91 MAN BECAUSE I BELIEVE
GOD IS MY SALVATION. GOD IS MY SPIRITUAL

BLESSING, MY PROSPERITY, MY HEALER, MY
DELIVERY, MY EVERYTHING THAT PERTAINS TO
LIFE AND GODLINESS.
REMEMBER IF THE HEART OF THE MATTER IS IN
THE HEART, THEN THERE IS NO OTHER PLACE
TO START FROM.
LEARN TO LET GO OF THE THINGS THAT YOU
CAN'T HELP, AND GRAB AHOLD OF THE THINGS
YOU CAN HELP.
YOU CAN LOVE AND HELP PEOPLE WITHOUT
COMPROMISING THE TRUTH OF GOD'S WORD.
GOD MUST BE FIRST AND NOT ASLEFTOVERS.
MY VALIDATION COMES FROM GOD. YOU CAN'T
STAND AT THE BUS STOP OF FAILURE, LOOKING
FOR THE SUCCESS BUS BECAUSE IT DOESN'T RUN
THAT ROUTE.
WHEN SHARING THE GOD IN YOU, YOU EXTEND
THE GOD IN YOU TO OTHERS. WHEN YOU
SHARE, YOU EXTEND BEYOUND YOU.
BEING RESPONSIBLE MEANS HAVING NO
EXCUSES TO RELY ON. WE HAVE THE GRACE TO
WHAT I CALL P.O.R.A.: PURSUE, OVERTAKE,
RECOVER, ALL.

AS CHRISTIANS, WE MUST BE WILLING TO
ACCEPT THE TRUTH THAT WE ARE CALLED TO
FORGIVE.

OUR COMMITMENT MUST BE TO GOD FIRST,
THEN FAMILY, CHURCH AND OTHERS.

THERE IS NO EXCUSES FOR FAILURE EVEN
THOUGH THERE ARE REASONS WHY PEOPLE
FAIL. REASONS CAN BE JUSTIFIED BECAUSE
NOTHING JUST HAPPENS, BUT EXCUSES CAN'T BE
JUSTIFIED BECAUSE YOU HAD A CHOICE.

I BELIEVE GRACE HAS ALWAYS EXISTED, BUT
HAS NOT ALWAYS BEEN PREACHED, TAUGHT, OR
LIVED BY.

NOW WE HEAR THE MESSAGE OF GRACE
TAUGHT AND LIVED BY MANY. YET THAT SAME
GRACE MESSAGE HAS BEEN WATERED DOWN BY
TRADITION AND RELIGION BECAUSE OF A FEAR
OF LOSING MEMBERS, FRIENDS OR JUST
WANTING TO STICK WITH THE OLD WAY OF
DOING THINGS. IN OTHER WORDS, THE LAW.

TO SOME DEGREE I BELIEVE THAT EFFORTS OF
FAITH EQUAL RESTING IN GRACE, AND THE OF
EFFORTS OF FEAR EQUAL THE TRUSTING IN THE
LAW. WE MUST UNDERSTAND THAT EFFORT IS
NOT JUST ENERGY RELEASED, IT ALSO MEANS

TIME SPENT WITH THE ENERGY THAT IS
RELEASED.

REMEMBER, SOME THINGS ARE DIFFICULT, BUT
POSSIBLE TO THOSE THAT BELIEVE.

WE LIVE IN A WORLD WHERE EXCUSES ARE
USED TO AVOID PERSONAL RESPONSIBILITY
AND TO DEFLECT BLAME.

ALL EXCUSES WERE NAILED TO THE CROSS WITH
JESUS AND LEFT THEM THERE SO THAT IT
WOULD BE POSSIBLE TO MAKE IT IN LIFE
DESPITE DIFFICULT CIRCUMSTANCES.

CHRISTIANS HAVE THE ADVANTAGE BECAUSE
OF JESUS IN THEIR LIVES. WITHOUT HIM WE ARE
ALL DOOMED AND HELL-BOUND. BELIEVERS
MUST RULE IN THE SPIRITUAL AND BE
INTOLERANT OF SICKNESS, LACK, POVERTY,
HATRED AND ANYTHING THAT IS CONTRARY TO
THE FRUIT OF THE SPIRIT.

CREATION BEGAN WITH AN IMAGE. GOD SAW
DARKNESS AND SPOKE LIGHT. GOD SAW
EVERYTHING HE SPOKE THAT WASN'T THERE
AND IT APPEARED BECAUSE GOD HIMSELF
CALLED THOSE THINGS THAT BE NOT AS
THOUGH THEY WERE.

WE AS BELIEVERS HAVE ALL THE ADVANAGE IN THIS LIFE AS LONG AS WE DON'T LET EXCUSES BECOME AN IMPERSONATOR OF REALITY, REFUSING ACCEPTANCE AND RESPONSIBILITY. WANTING MORE THINGS IN LIFE FOR THE WRONG REASON IS CALLED GREED AND WANTING LESS IN LIFE FOR THE WRONG REASON IS CALLED SELFISHNESS. GOD HAS DONE ALL THAT HE IS GOING TO DO IN OUR LIVES AND WE MUST ACCEPT ALL THAT HE HAS DONE.

SINCE COMPLAINING AND MURMURING IS A SIN, THE BEST WAY OUT OF BOTH IS TO START BEING APPRECIATIVE, GRATEFUL AND THANKFUL. LET US START TRAINING IN THE SPIRITUAL NFL =NEVER FAILING LIFE.

LIVING A SPIRIT-FILLED LIFE IN THE LOVE OF GOD IS NOT FAILURE BUT A CHALLENGE. YOU CAN NEVER FAIL AT ANYTHING YOU HAVEN'T STARTED, BECAUSE ZERO ATTEMPTS=ZERO COMPLETIONS. SINCE LIFE IS SAID TO BE HOW WE SEE IT, THEN WHAT ARE YOU LOOKING AT? EVERYBODY HAS A PHILOSOPHY THAT COULD EITHER BE WRONG OR RIGHT BUT IF IT IS TIED TO THE WORD OF GOD IT IS RIGHT REGARDLESS

OF WHAT MIGHT LOOK LIKE A DISCREPANCY. THE ONLY TRUTH YOU DON'T WANT TO HEAR IS THE TRUTH YOU DON'T WANT TO CHANGE.

THE BIBLE SAYS TO WRITE THE VISION AND MAKE IT PLAIN ON TABLETS THAT HE MAY RUN THAT READ IT. SO LET US WRITE, READ, AND RUN WITH THE VISION GOD HAS GIVEN US AS CHRISTIANS!

REMEMBER WE ARE AGREEING WITH WHAT IS BEING SAID WHEN WE DO WHAT IS BEING SAID. WALKING IN THE LOVE OF GOD IS WALKING IN INTEGRITY (NUMBERS 23:19). YOU CAN ONLY BE DENIED WHEN YOU LIVE IN DENIAL AND YOU CAN ONLY BE STOPPED WHEN YOU BELIEVE WHAT YOU SEE OVER WHAT THE WORD SAYS AND/OR BELIEVE IT IS WHAT YOU DESERVE. WE KNOW THAT THERE ARE 5 SENSES, SOMETIME REFERRED TO AS PHYSICAL SENSES. THERE ARE ALSO 5 SPIRITUAL SENSES TO CORRALATE WITH THOSE 5 BASIC SENSES. THERE ARE ANSWERS WAITING IN THE PRESENCE OF THE LORD

BUT WE MUST BE IN THE PRESENCE TO GET THOSE ANSWERS.

THE FIRST RESPONDERS OF LIFE WERE THE WORDS OF LIFE, IN THAT CREATION STARTED WITH WORDS. IF YOU DON'T KNOW THAT, IT WOULD BE WISE NOT TO COMMENT ON IT BECAUSE ONE OF THE BEST WAYS TO EXPRESS IGNORANCE IS TRYING TO EXPLAIN A WISDOM OF WHICH YOU KNOW NOTHING ABOUT. ONE OF THE MOST POWERFUL STATEMENTS IN THE BIBLE IS GALATIANS 5:6 WHICH SAYS, "IN CHRIST JESUS NEITHER CIRCUMCISION NOR UNCIRCUMCISION HAS ANY VALUE BUT FAITH WHICH WORKETH BY LOVE." THESE TWO WORDS, LOVE AND FAITH ARE VALUABLE LIKE BLOOD AND WATER.

AS BELIEVERS WE ARE NOT IN CONTROL BECAUSE WE HAVE GREAT WEALTH AND ALL THE EXTERNAL SUCCESS BUT ONLY WHEN WE LET THE CREATOR OF WEALTH CONTROL OUR LIFE AND DESTINY, REMEMBER TRUE WEALTH AND SUCCESS BEGIN INTERNALLY. IT IS SEEN WITH THE SPIRITUAL EYE AND THEN THE NATURAL EYE. PROGRESS MEANS MOVING FORWARD AND CONTRARILY REGRESSION IS THE A STATE OF GOING BACKWARDS OR RECLINING TO A LESSOR POSITION. OUR TOTAL

EXISTENCE IS BASED UPON THE IMAGE WE SEE IN OURSELVES AS CHILDREN OF GOD. THIS PART OF OUR LIFE IN THIS EXISTENCE HAS A TIME LIMIT BUT THE PART OF OUR LIVES OUTSIDE THIS EXISTENCE IS IN ETERNITY WHICH HAS NO TIME AND NO LIMIT BECAUSE WE ARE BORN NATURALLY BUT BORN AGAIN SPIRITUALLY. LIFE HAS NO BIRTHDAY NEITHER DOES ETERNITY. JESUS IS OUR LIFE.

REMEMBER, DON'T STAND AT THE BUS STOP OF FAILURE LOOKING FOR THE SUCCESS BUS BECAUSE IT DOESN'T RUN THAT ROUTE. THERE ARE EXCUSES FOR MISSING OUT! THE BIBLE SAYS THAT WISDOM IS THE PRINCIPAL THING; THEREFORE, GET WISDOM, AND IN ALL YOUR GETTING, GET UNDERSTANDING. (PROVERB 4:7)

THERE IS NO WISDOM IN THE GRAVE ACCORDING TO ECCLESIASTES 9:10 THERE IS ALSO NO WORK, DEVICE, KNOWLEDGE, NOR WISDOM IN THE GRAVE BUT THAT WHATEVER WE FIND TO DO WITH OUR HANDS DO IT WITH ALL OUR MIGHT.

WE HAVE BEEN TAUGHT THAT THE MIND IS THE ARENA OF FAITH AND THAT BEING SAID AN

ARENA IS WHERE FIGHTS TAKE PLACE. LIKE PAUL SAID WE FIGHT THE GOOD FIGHT OF FAITH AND TAKE HOLD OR LAY HOLD ON ETERNAL LIFE WHICH GOD HAS CALLED USTO. FIGHTING THE GOOD FIGHT MEANS YOU WIN. ROMANS 12:21 SAYS DO NOT BE OVERCOME BY EVIL BUT OVERCOME EVIL WITH GOOD. THE GOOD THAT WE OVERCOME THE EVIL WITH IS GOD'S WORD IN FAITH & LOVE. WE CAN TURN EVIL INTO A GOOD LIFE! (EVIL SPELLED BACKWARDS IS LIVE. AND, IF WE SPELL THE WORD DEVIL BACKWARDS, WE GET THE WORD LIVED.)

08.2019

Untitled

WE AS BORN-AGAIN BELIEVERS MUST
UNDERSTAND THAT THE IMAGE WE HAVE OF
OUR LIVES WILL BECOME THE REALITY OF OUR
LIVES ACCORDING TO GENESIS CHAPTER 11:6.
JUST BECAUSE EVIL HAS A CONFERENCE CALL,
DOESN'T MEAN YOU CAN'T DENY THE
INVITATION TO ANSWER OR ATTEND. THE BIBLE
SAYS THAT IT IS BETTER TO GIVE THAN TO
RECEIVE, BUT IT DOESN'T SAY DON'T RECEIVE.
THE BEST WAY TO GIVE SOMETHING OF VALUE
TO YOURSELF IS TO GIVE SOMETHING OF VALUE
TO OTHERS FIRST.
AS CHRISTIANS, WHEN WE WITNESS TO PEOPLE
THAT ARE NOT BORN AGAIN, WE ARE HEARD BY
WHAT WE SAY AND NOTICED BY WHAT WE DO.
WE CAN'T LEAD SINNERS TO CHRIST IF WE
HAVEN'T BEEN LED TO CHRIST.
THE WORD KEEPS ON DOING WHAT IT HAS
ALWAYS DONE AND IT'S ALL GOOD.
GOD'S WORD NEVER CHANGES. THERE HAS
BEEN NO CHANGE IN THE WORD, AND
THEREFORE NO CHANGE TO MY HEALING, MY
DELIVERANCE AND ALL THAT GOD HAS
PROMISED. IT IS ALL STILL INTACT.

THE LAW HAS NOT CHANGED NEITHER HAS
GRACE, BUT WE AS BELIEVERS MUST
UNDERSTAND THE DIFFERENCE BETWEEN THE
TWO.

JESUS SAID MY GRACE IS SUFFICIENT FOR YOU
BECAUSE MY STRENGTH IS MADE PERFECT IN
YOUR WEAKNESS. REMEMBER, LET THE WEAK
SAY I AM STRONG AND LET THE POOR SAY I AM
RICH. FOR WHAT THE LORD HAS DONE FOR US,
LET'S GIVE THANKS.

LOVE IS THE ESSENCE OR INDISPENSABLE
MORAL QUALITY OF GOD HIMSELF, THE
CREATOR OF HEAVEN, EARTH AND LIFE ITSELF.
THE FRUIT OF THE SPIRIT CANNOT EXIST
WITHOUT FAITH & LOVE BECAUSE FAITH WORKS
BY LOVE ACCORDING TO GALATIANS 5:6. FOR IN
JESUS, NEITHER CIRCUMCISION NOR
UNCIRCUMCISION HAS ANY VALUE. ON THE
TREE OF LOVE HANGS ALL THE OTHER FRUIT:
JOY, PEACE, PATIENCE, KINDNESS, GOODNESS,
FAITHFULNESS, GENTLENESS, AND
SELF- CONTROL, AGAINST SUCH FRUIT THERE IS
NO LAW.

THERE IS NOTHING THAT CAN CONQUER WHAT
CAN'T FAIL AND LOVE IS THE "MORE THAN A

CONQUEROR" THAT CANNOT FAIL BECAUSE GOD IS LOVE. (ROMANS 8:37-39) THERE IS NO FEAR IN LOVE BECAUSE PERFECT LOVE CASTS OUT FEAR. THEREFORE, WE MUST LET LOVE CAST OUT THE PUNISHMENT THAT COMES WITH OPERATING IN FEAR. GOD IS LOVE AND OUR PROTECTION, OUR SHIELD, OUR DEFENSE AND OUR SHELTER FROM THE SPIRIT OF FEAR (1 JOHN 4:18)

This Day

THIS DAY IS NOT YESTERDAY, THIS DAY IS NOT TOMORROW.
THIS DAY IS TODAY, FILLED WITH LAUGHTER, JOY, NOT SORROW.
THIS DAY IS HERE, LET US ENJOY ALL THAT'S IN IT.
THIS DAY GOD GAVE TO ME & I WON'T WASTE A MINUTE.
THIS DAY I'LL WORSHIP THE FATHER, SON, & HOLY GHOST.
THIS DAY I'LL PRAISE THE CREATER& SAVIOUR WHO LOVE ME MOST.
THIS DAY IS MY DAY TO GIVE THANKS MORE THAN I'VE EVER DONE.
THIS DAY I'LL WALK IN LOVE UNTIL THE GOING DOWN OF THE SUN.
THIS DAY I WILL PRAY AND STUDY GOD'S HOLY WORD.
THIS DAY I WILL MAKE NO EXCUSES; I'VE LEARNED, received, AND HEARD.
THIS DAY IS ONLY TODAY AND WILL NEVER BE ANY MORE.
THIS DAY IS MY DAY TO BE LIKE EAGLE AND SOAR.

09.10.1998

I'm Determined

I'm determined to walk in love no matter what it takes.
I'm determined to walk in love no matter the mistakes.
I'm determined to walk in love each and every day.
I'm determined to walk in love no matter what people say.
I'm determined to walk in love no matter what people do.
I'm determined to walk in love because the Word says to.
I'm determined to walk in love no matter how I feel.
I'm determined to walk in love because it is God's will.
I'm determined to walk in love because love never fails.
I'm determined to walk in love for by my walk, people can tell.
I'm determined to walk in love because love will see me through.
I'm determined to walk in love to see the greater one in you.
I'm determined to walk in love because love does no wrong.
I'm determined to walk in love because love makes me strong.
I'm determined to walk in love because love is not a hater.
I'm determined to walk in love because I know nothing greater.

Beyond This Point

BEYOND THIS POINT START YOUR FUTURE BECAUSE ALL THAT IS AHEAD OF YOU IS IN FRONT OF YOU. CHOICE IS YOUR FUTURE BECAUSE IT IS THE DECISION THAT YOU HAVE CHOSEN.

BEYOND THIS POINT ALL EXPECTATIONS MUST BE ACTED UPON IN ORDER FOR ANYTHING TO BE ACCOMPLISH.

THE TERM FUTURE MEANS PROSPECT, OUTLOOK, UPCOMING, POTENTIAL, HOPE, OPPORTUNITY, YET TO COME.

SO, BEYOND THIS POINT IN YOUR LIFE IS HOPE, OPPORTUNITY, YET TO COME, OUTLOOK, AND UPCOMING POTENTIAL.

MANY WORDS WILL BE SPOKEN AND MANY THOUGHTS WILL BE THOUGHT, BUT BEYOND THIS POINT THE OUTCOME WILL BE DETERMINE BY WHAT YOU DO NOW.

AT THIS POINT IN YOUR LIFE WILL BRING WHAT IS BEYOND THIS POINT IN YOUR LIFE. LIFE IS A SUBJECT WITH AN ENDLESS DISCUSSION.

YOUR FUTURE IS IN WHAT YOU DO NOW NOT IN WHAT YOU DO LATER.

PREPARATION IS FOR RESULTS AND RESULTS IS THE FRUIT OF PREPARATION. FRUITLESS PLANNING EQUALS A FRUITLESS FUTURE

YOU WILL NEVER GET AHEAD IN LIFE IF YOU DON'T PLAN AHEAD FOR LIFE.

THE IMAGE GOD HAS OF YOU IS ENDLESS BECAUSE YOU WERE MADE IN HIS IMAGE AND LIKENESS BY THE INFINITE GOD HIMSELF.

WHEN YOU DON'T CARE OR SAY OTHER'S DON'T MATTER, IT MEANS YOU HAVE STARTED A SELFISH WITNESS TRAIL THAT LEADS TO THE PATH OF DESTRUCTION.

BEYOND THIS POINT IS WHAT WE CALL THE GOLDEN RULE. LOVE IS THAT GOLDEN RULE. LOVE IS THE AXLE THAT THE WORLD IS CARRIED AROUND ON.

IF YOU TRY TO DEFEAT WHAT IS BEHIND YOU, YOU WILL BE DEFEATED BY WHAT IS BEFORE YOU.

PROPER PROSPECTIVE IS THE KEY TO RIGHTEOUS JUDGEMENT.

PERHAPS YOU ARE WONDERING WHAT I MEAN BY BEYOND THIS POINT. I MEAN THAT YOUR LIFE IS AN EXTENTION BEYOND WHERE YOU ARE NOW IN LIFE. DON'T ALWAYS LOOK AT NOW, LOOK AHEAD OF NOW SO YOU WILL BE ON YOUR WAY TO WHERE YOU WANT TO GO.

BEYOND THIS POINT IS WISDOM FROM ON HIGH.

BEYOND THIS POINT IS THE LOVE OF GOD.

BEYOND THIS POINT NO ONE IS GREATER THAN THEIR ATTITUDE ASSUMED.

BEYOND THIS POINT WILL BE THE END OF WHERE YOU STARTED FROM.

BEYOND THIS POINT IS ENDLESS POTENTIAL FUELING YOUR BEGINNING.

BEYOND THIS POINT YOU MUST CONTINUE INSPITE OF ANY OBSTACLES.

BEYOND THIS POINT SIN IS ITS OWN STRENGTH, AND LOVE IS ITS OWN VICTORY

BEYOND THIS POINT IS THE PATH THAT LEADS TO YOUR DESTINY.

BEYOND THIS POINT, WHAT ARE YOU LOOKING FOR?

BEYOND THIS POINT IS ALL ANSWERS TO ALL QUESTIONS.

BEYOND THIS POINT ARE YOU ASKING QUESTIONS OR ARE YOU SEEKING ANSWERS?

BEYOND THE DESPERATE REACH IS THE REACHABLE BECAUSE OF DETERMINATION

WE MUST BELIEVE THAT WE RECEIVE ALL THAT IS AVAILABLE TO US AS HEIRS.

BEYOND IS NEVER IN ITS PLACE IT IS FARTHER THAN HERE. HERE IS PRESENT, BEYOND IS FUTURE.

BEYOND THIS POINT YOU CAN NEVER WALK THE SPIRITUAL PATH OF GOD IF YOU ARE ALWAYS WEIGHTED DOWN WITH YOUR OWN SELFISH SENSE OF IMPORTANCE.

IF A MAN CAN'T CARRY HIS OWN WEIGHT OF CONCERN FOR OTHERS, THEN HE MUST BE A DEPENDENT UPON OTHERS.

LOVE AND FAITH IS THE PASSPORT TO YOUR SUCCESSFUL DESTINATION CALLED LIFE.

THE POINT OF INTEREST FOR EVERY CHRISTIAN SHOULD BE A SUCCESSFUL, GODLY LIFE. WHY WOULD ANYTHING ELSE IN LIFE BE OF INTEREST TO YOU EXCEPT BEING A BLESSING TO OTHERS?

HONESTY AND INTEGRITY PLAY A MAJOR ROLL IN HAVING A PROSPEROUS LIFE, SOMETHING MOST TEND TO IGNORE.

BEYOND HATE IS THE LOVE OF GOD ILLUMINATED IN OUR HEARTS BY THE HOLY GHOST.

BEYOND LACK IS THE ABUNDANCE OF GOD IN OUR LIVES. BEYOND SICKNESS IS DIVINE HEALTH. BEYOND POVERTY IS PROSPERITY. BEYOND DESPAIR IS HOPE.

BEYOND WHAT WE CAN'T SEE IS THE VISIBLE.

BEYOND THE IMPOSSIBLE WITH MAN IS THE POSSIBLE WITH GOD.

BEYOND GOD THERE IS NOTHING ELSE, FOR GOD IS ALL THERE IS.

07.31.2005

Beyond the Horizon of Reasoning

Wisdom is the principal thing because it is the Word of God. Beyond human reasoning is the wisdom of God that can only be obtained by studying the Word for revelation knowledge.

Revealed knowledge is beyond sense knowledge. Beyond the horizonal reasoning of man is the wisdom of God in the form of a vertical relationship. The Bible tells us in 1st Corinthians Chapter 2: 1-77 about spiritual wisdom.

When a man tries to reason with God, he is asking God to compromise His Word which God CAN NOT do.

The wisdom of God is always accurate while compromising

is without standard.

The wisdom of God is the Word of God and the will of God is for every man to abide in His Word.

Wisdom is the ability to create and enhance sense knowledge.

Reasoning is like a commercial, a constant interruption to the original purpose of the Word.

Remember, wisdom is the is principal thing, not reasoning.

Wisdom sees answers through faith and faith is the substance of creative matter and belief is the weaver of accomplishments.

Looking beyond the horizon of reasoning is to expect something greater than an ordinary way of life.

Beyond is like potential which is endless when you recognize it is not where you stop.

All physical matter came from spiritual matter and God created all matter. Spiritually speaking, you can speak life or death to any physical thing.

For example, Jesus spoke to a physical fig tree and it dried up from the root. And He spoke to the wind, rain, and literal mountains and they obeyed him.

Sense knowledge is what you know. Revealed knowledge is what you understand as the result of intimacy with God.

The horizontal is as far as you can see naturally but the vertical is further than we can see supernaturally.

Many religious leaders reasoned amongst themselves when they questioned Jesus about why He was saying and doing what He said and did.

Beyond reasoning is the wisdom of God.

Beyond head knowledge is the wisdom of God.

Beyond educational intellect is the wisdom of God.

Beyond the letter of the law is the law of the spirit of life in Christ Jesus which has made me [us] free from the law of sin and death. Wisdom was in the beginning at the time of creation. When God said let there be light, wisdom was involved in the process. Behind every "let there be" was an action.

When God spoke, whatever He spoke was already done because God spoke the end from the beginning.

Beyond the horizon of reasoning is wisdom because wisdom is the key that unlocks all complications.

Wisdom requests that we seek her at all times and in any situation because wisdom is the Word of God.

Wisdom is the main ingredient in our love walk.

The wisdom of the Lord is beyond measure in our lives. Beyond what we can imagine, think, say, or do is both the wisdom of God and the love of God.

The wisdom of God activated in our lives is greater than our decisions without it.

Reasoning is mostly the result of those who have their own opinions and are not subject to listening to those with wisdom.

The Bible says in Proverbs chapter 1:7 that a fool despises wisdom and instruction. Ecclesiastes7:9 says be not hasty in thy spirit to be angry, for anger resteth in the bosom of fools. There is no reasoning nor wisdom in anger.

The word will always go against man's reasoning and rationalizations in his own mind.

When it is God, it will require faith and courage and it will align with the Word of God.

God is all there is and there is no other true God but God trying to separate God from his Word is like trying to separate water from water. No matter how much you get from the source it will remain what it is.

In James 1:5, it says if any of you lack wisdom, let him ask of God that giveth to all men liberally, and upbraideth not; and it[wisdom] shall be given him.

Beyond the horizon of reasoning, God is able to do exceedingly, abundantly above all that we ask or think, according to the power that worketh in us. [Ephesians 3:20]

Man's reasoning is no comparison to God's wisdom. In Mark 2:6, while the scribes were reasoning in their hearts, Jesus perceived in His spirit that they reasoned within themselves, and asked "why reason ye these things in your hearts?" This was because Jesus had healed a paralyzed man and said "son, thy sins be forgiven thee."

In Mark 12:28 and Luke 9:46, they begin to question Jesus about things He was saying that they could not perceive in their minds.

Beyond the horizon of reasoning, wisdom perceives what reasoning tries to justify. Wisdom is beyond what is reasonable and justifiable because it is the Word of God.

God's Word is always pregnant with information and revelation and will never run out of either one.

Information gets you to the source. but revelation gets you in the source to receive invaluable information.

Since life is a series of decisions, you must make one to determine your destiny in life.

Wisdom recognizes that love is the key that overrides hatred.

Hatred is the result of selfishness and selfishness is the result of lack.

01.24.2005

Special Thanks

I would like to thank my three children for their love and support. They mean everything to me.

About the Author

James Jackson is father to three adult children whose love and support mean everything to him. Mr. Jackson is a 30+ year member of World Changers Church International, College Park, GA where he has been taught the Word of God with simplicity and understanding under the teachings of Dr. Creflo A. Dollar.

Mr. Jackson knows that although nothing in life is easy, we can do all things through and with Jesus Christ. If you do not know Jesus, He is waiting on you to admit your sin, confess and accept Him as your Savior and Lord. This is done by a desire to change by confessing Romans 10:9,10 followed by Romans12:2. All this was made possible by John 3:16. Do it now!

Contact: leejackson1903@gmail.com

Made in the USA
Columbia, SC
30 August 2023

22244043R00046